An Angel for You

My Life in Poems, Letters & Short Stories

By Chris the "Abducted Alien"

2007

*There is no Greater agony...
than bearing an untold story inside you.*

Maya Angelou

Disclaimer: All last names of living authors of some of the verses, poems, or letters have not been shown to protect living people and their family members. All poems in this book are the property of the respective poets and are duly noted by name and copyright. Copyrights have been searched and included on the credits and resource page for verses and phrases used in this book. Should anyone recognize any information or graphics used in this book as theirs please contact me at: Chris_the_Abducted_Alien@comcast.net (2007).

ISBN: 978-0-6151-7021-3

Copyright © 2007 by Chris the "Abducted Alien"
All rights reserved, including the right to reproduce in whole or in part in any form.

To my Love Felicia, whose enthusiasm and love at a crucial stage...
Is more important than she knows!

To my parents and all the people I have loved...
and who have loved me in my lifetime.

Never a lip is curved in pain
That can't be kissed into smiles again[1]!

Bret Harte

Volume 1
2nd Edition

This book is dedicated to **Sondra Lee Y**...my first true love and one
of my first teachers in the meaning of love and life.

Born 1950 – Died June 4, 2000

I'm sorry I could not tell you before you left this earth.

You were the greatest influence in my life!

There is no passion greater than the one that touches-not the body-but the heart.

---

[1] American writer who helped create the local-colour school in American fiction. (1836-1902)

Author's Introduction

I was told in 1969 by my close friend Bonnie who was a psychic...

"Your love relationships will not go well in your life; there will be a lot of tragedy in your love life. And it will be difficult to keep a relationship with any one person. You will continue to find love and lose it."

I did not know what she meant back then, but I understand it today.

People you thought would never hurt you in your life will. And you will be left to think about "WHY?"

You will hurt others and have to carry the pain with you for a lifetime, and you will ask yourself "WHY?"

Most people will not accept other people for who or what they are, and they try to change them so the relationship will be compatible. If people are not compatible in a relationship, it does not matter how much they try...it never works when people try to change who or what they are.

I have tried to change for some of the loves in my life, only to realize it was not me. But I would always ask myself, *"Well who am I then? And what do I want out of a relationship?"*

I continue to watch the relationships of others in my life. Everyone has his or her own story to tell. But I always wonder about the relationships where two people have been together for decades.

The few people in these relationships are happy and content. Others are miserable, yet they continue their relationship.

I have finally come to realize that all I want in life is to be happy. But I could never find a person to be with who would allow me to have this in any relationship.

I have constantly struggled to attain happiness, both personal and professional, throughout my life.

However, both people and events have tried to prevent me from attaining this happiness.

Is this only *my* life that happiness cannot be attained, or has this just been *my* life's destiny?

Chris the "Abducted Alien" 2007

Editor's Comment

I am telling you now, as a friend in 2007, that you can still prove Bonnie wrong. The future is like our class schedules – always tentative.

Always ask why...because what you know does not matter if you do not understand it.

Do not believe that destiny is set in stone. Instead, remember that a stone can be broken and shaped into something new.

Copyright © September 8, 2007 – Anthony Paul Manno

Acknowledgments

This book emerged from years of feeling that something was missing. My inability to feel the love as others did towards me...and when I was the one that felt love, the other did not.

I want to thank Felicia for being true of heart and allowing me to truly believe that two people can find true love in life together.

I would also like to thank all the people in my life who have given me the opportunity to truly see that I have been loved. I now have the capacity to return that love to someone. It took a long time, but I am truly grateful to all of you.

Thank you to my mother, Helene, for giving me kind and loving moral values in my life. I will always remember your love and beautiful smile.

Thank you to my sister Evelyn for having a kind and forgiving heart, and for putting up with me all this time.

To all four of my youngest sisters, I truly do love you all. And I am sorry that I could not find the time to show you.

I have now accepted all of my emotions, love lost and love found, and would like to share it with the world.

I hope you enjoy reading this compilation of poems, letters, and short stories from everyone who has touched my heart at some point during my life.

Chris the "Abducted Alien"

Table of Contents   **Page(s)**

Authors Introduction.. 4-5
Editors Comment
***
Acknowledgments.. 6
***
Kaleidoscope of My Mind.................................. 11-13
Whirlwind
***
Angels Without Wings.. 14-15
***
Ritual Tea with Chris.. 16-17
***
The Clouds... 18-19
***
My Dear Chris.. 20-24
***
Broken Heart.. 25
***
My Wish for You.. 26
***
Forgive My Heart... 27
***
The Mind's Eye.. 28
***
Pity Me Not.. 29
***
The Beautiful In Life.. 30
***
Love Is For Me... 31
***
How Much for Love?... 32
***
Here I Am... 33
***
Tick-Tock.. 34
Alone Again

Table of Contents	**Page(s)**
The Christmas Story………………………………	35
Forever's End………………………………………..	36
What Is Love? ……………………………………….	37
If I Knew…………………………………………..	38-39
Just My Thoughts of You…………………………	40
My Love's Passion…………………………………..	41
Felicia……………………………………………....	42
Where Have All the Butterflies Gone?……………	43-44
Since I Met You……………………………………	45
She……………………………………………….......	46
Love Is……………………………………………..	47
We Is Friends! …………………………………….....	48
A Special World…………………………………...	49
One Heart…………………………………………	50
What I Love About You…………………………..	51
October's Party………………………....................	52
My Goodbye…………………………………….....	53
To Master Love……………………………………	54
I Will Surrender Only To You…………………….	55-57

(*** separators appear between each entry)

Table of Contents   **Page(s)**

My Angel, My Confusion…………………….   58-60
To Sandy
***

Silence……………………………………….   61
***

My Daddy……………………………………..   62
***

You Are the One Who………………………...   63
***

The Wind, the Sand, and the Sky…………….   64
***

Dwelling on Past Pain………………………...   65
***

Happiness Is the Road………………………..   66
***

My Feelings…………………………………..   67
***

She Is More Than a Lover……………………   68
***

Love's Sacrifice……………………………….   69
***

Pity Me Not…………………………………   70
Anguished Love
***

Soupir d'amour (Whisper of Love)...........................   71
Sorrow
***

Time to Go…………………………………..   72-73
***

Dion – Dedicated to Our Family and Friends……….   74
***

Shari……………………………………….....   75
***

Fulfilled……………………………………….   76
***

Deep Breath………………………………........   77

Table of Contents   **Page(s)**

Because of You…………………………………....   78
***
The Voice of a Friend (Trees of Life)…………….....   79
***
Ode to My Family………………………………...   80
***
You and I………………………………………….   81-82
***
Rebound Lover…………………………………...   83-86
***
Come to the End of Words………………………..   87
***
Till We Meet Again………………………………..   88
***
Credits and Sources………………………………..   89-91

Kaleidoscope of My Mind

A radical is one who speaks the truth.

Charles A. Lindbergh

It is better to be faithful than famous.

Theodore Roosevelt

A happy family is but an earlier heaven.

John Bowring

Paternity is a career imposed on you without any inquiry into your fitness.

Adlie E. Stevenson

Your life is an unfolding mystery, be humble in your perpetual uncertainty.

- Paul Pearsall in Making Miracles

Treasure the ones that truly care, release the ones that don't know how.

Author Unknown

Kaleidoscope of My Mind

We must be willing to change our life now in order for a new life to begin in this lifetime.

Author Unknown

Just feel, don't think and the words will come.

Chris the "Abducted Alien", 2006

A true heart and honesty....will bring you true love in your lifetime.

Chris the "Abducted Alien", 2006

Obstacles are part of your life, enjoy them while you can…the only other option is to die!

Chris the "Abducted Alien", 2007

Someone once said…

Ours is not to reason why, ours is to do or die!

I truly believe this now, I am living proof…

2007

Kaleidoscope of My Mind

I am guilty of all the good I could have done in life and did not do, now's the time to do it!

Chris the "Abducted Alien"

I have always tried my best to stay away from conflict in my life, whether it was the right thing to do at the time or not. I do not consciously think about what I am doing at the time it is happening, it just has always been a part of me and what was happening at that moment in time.

I would live my life in a box and not feel anyone or anything else around me. I would forget about all the problems and failures in my life. This was a protective device against pain. I lived this way for a long time. But not anymore!

Chris the "Abducted Alien", 2006

Whirlwind

The ensuing crisis can be a turning point for our
relationship or love life,
But, only if you are willing to let go and take that
chance...many people are not!

Author Unknown

Angels Without Wings[2]

What are angels? They are whatever we want them to be. Angels are all around us. All we have to do is stop and feel. Some of us are too cynical or busy to notice. Some think they have wings, but others will not even acknowledge their existence.

They, in fact, are no different than you and I. Angels take many shapes and forms. They have lived and are now part of our souls. Others are living right before our eyes and we do not even realize it. They are waiting to assist us with our lives and problems. They talk to us when we need help or are lonely. And when we are happy, they are happy with us.

Our hearts must be pure to receive all of this love. Then we can say, *"Maybe they were sent from above!"*

But whatever the situation is, angels are here only to guide us. They do not work for us. We make things in life happen because we listen to their advice and follow the

---

[2] This short story is also included in my book "Abducted Alien: A True Story of United States Immigration" is tentatively scheduled for mid 2008 publication.

path they have given to us as an option. On earth, it is always our choice whether or not to follow that path.

But sometimes, they guide us without our conscious thoughts interfering with the many choices. This is when we should thank them for leading us in the right direction.

When I have nowhere to turn or go…when there is no one to talk to and I am feeling kind of low, I search deep within myself--for it is the love inside my heart that lets me know my Angels are there with me, even though we are a universe apart!

Chris, the "Abducted Alien" (August 24, 2007)

Ritual Tea with Chris

Opening the door, we feel the hot air rush past us and into the hallway.

At first, it feels good after the cold, night air. Then it is too hot.

As she opens the windows, I light candles and prepare the tea. This has become our nightly ritual.

After serving her tea, I pour myself a glass of wine. I usually reserve this ancient ritual for solitude, but the night is much too warm for hot tea.

Filling my favorite pipe with flower tops, I relax in a chair and wait patiently for the soothing effects of marijuana to take over.

The room is slowly filling with cool night air that makes the candles dance and the leaves of the plants prance softly on the gentle breeze.

Figures emerge from light and non-light and play gaily on the walls and ceiling.

Good little spirits transcend dimension after dimension, being and not being, seeing and not seeing, feeling and not feeling…they transcend all.

It is an unusual time, a different time…than any other time before. We all know it, see it, feel it…but we can't say it, even though it needs to be said.

I stare out the window and try to pretend that it isn't so. There is no right time, no knowing time, no time that when things unborn or unheard of emerge from the depths of infinity never to be hidden again. And yet…I know that it is so and can never be otherwise…for it is now, and not yesterday or tomorrow, that I realize the difference her presence makes.

I sit next to her and we talk of things neither to be taken seriously nor to be regarded as mere idle conversation.

I want to tell her…but I want to be sure; for there is no room for half truths.

I look into her eyes and the desire to speak is replaced by the desire to feel…and I know…I truly know that I care for her.

The candles dance and the images prance around the tiny room, while the leaves of the plants sway in the breeze and I lie staring into a beautiful dream of future nights…and ritual tea.

Written by: Sondra Lee Y…   1974

The Clouds

I awoke this morning to find your head on my shoulder, your leg crossing mine, your arm touching mine, your breath warm and moist on my neck.
Your soft brown hair whirling and twirling in a hundred different ways…

Your lips are so soft and warm on my skin.

I want to crush you to my breast and feel your heart beat next to mine.

If I were an artist, I'd paint you a thousand times.

If I were a poet, I'd write you a million lines.

Artist I'll never be, poet…well possibly…all the way through infinity.

I place my hand on your face and run my fingers through your hair.

You continue to sleep and let the world take care…

I look at you and wonder what it is that someone as beautiful as you could ever see in me.

Every time you say to me "I love you" I want to say it too!

I feel such a desperate need to say it, but without feeling it, what can I do?

I have this fear of hurting you, which is something I never want to do.

What if I can't love you (here we are again) what am I suppose to do?

Sometimes I feel like a person with no beginning and no end…

Life goes by me so slowly, but I'm always on the outside looking in.

I feel your lashes brush so softly against my cheek.

I raise my head and look at you; I feel so sad and incomplete.

Your eyes say so much that I can't understand…

It's as though we are worlds apart and I'm still on the outside…looking in.

What is it that you can see that enables you to love someone as vague as me?

Can it possibly be, that you can see the real me…which even I can't see?

My head touches your face…you smile…

I think I'm soaring above the clouds…!

Written by: Sondra Lee Y…   *January 16, 1975*

My Dear Chris

How or why you put up with me, and how or why I put up with the same thing you've been experiencing now for three years is beyond my comprehension. Although you don't say it in plain terms, I imagine that I make you feel inferior and taken for granted. I know this is going to sound ironic, but the <u>only</u> reason I treat you this way is because I really do love you and want to be with you for as long as living together makes us both happy.

People have taken me for granted all of my life. They <u>assume</u> that because I look the way I do, that I can <u>only</u> end up as an A, B, or C. And beyond these given choices, I do not exist. In other words, if I do not marry a doctor or a lawyer, or if I do not become a teacher or a social worker-- or some way, somehow fit into their social status bullshit, I am destined to be nothingness, an idiot, a welfare check receiver with ten kids. It was not until I hitch-hiked to California and told them to fuck-off that I don't need them, that I finally got some consideration as a person. And now that I have returned, no one is saying, "You should be this, or do that." They know that I am going to do <u>only what I want to do</u>.

I know this is going to sound like the thoughts of a deranged person; but in a way, I'm taking out my frustrations on you. Why? Because it seems to me that…you've been a person who has taken most people for granted, never bothering to find out what they are really like. Stepping on them and never caring. Taking and seldom giving, lying to spare feelings that you know will eventually come about.

It's like what goes around comes around; and in some twisted way, I am your karma. Here's a double twist; I also feel that I'm putting you through some sort of durability test. If you pass, you will emerge a stronger (mentally), more determined, and more confident person.

All of this is necessary as I will demonstrate below:

Four people are doing something in couples. Couple A) consists of #1 – A very strong and determined person and #2 – A willing, but not very confident person. Couple B) consists of #3 A strong determined person and Couple #4 – A very strong determined person.

Who will achieve their goal first, given all odds are even? Who will appreciate the struggle more and who will enjoy the results most?

I hope you get my point. But there's more! There are times when I become very bored, not with you or anything in particular. Just bored!

It's like nothing can satisfy me during these periods. I've been like this my whole life; I can't blame this on anyone. I believe it happens because I can all too easily settle for a position in life that is merely satisfying and not totally fulfilling. So when these periods intervene, I become determined to find something that will fulfill the desire I feel so intensely. This is sometimes worst than pain. So help me, I haven't the faintest idea what I truly desire. I know it has something to do with the ability to create. I'm not really sure in what form though.

I don't believe this is on a small scale, for I have dabbled in practically all art forms at one time or another. I think that it is something that will require a great deal of money and a lifetime of dedication. And I feel that without it I can never truly be a whole person.

I have long accepted the saying, *"A true artist doesn't only depict pain; he lives in it."* There is a lot that can be said for pain. Just as much, I believe, that can be said for love.

Chris, I have truly been alone all of my life; it's what you might call self-exile. I enjoy being alone, and it is only when I'm alone that I realize how very much I need you.

As long as I'm doing something, I'm okay. But when I'm idle, I become depressed. It is those times that I wish you were here; but on the other hand, I'm glad you're not because thinking about when you will be here is very important to me. "Absence makes the heart grow fonder," is very true for me. It's almost masochistic! I enjoy doing without because I enjoy it more when I finally get what I want. I like saving the best for last. The longer (within reason) that I save something, the better it is to me.

I am never worried; nor do I anticipate any financial help from you. I can see that you're doing <u>everything</u> possible to get money. But please don't put yourself too far out; we'll make it; we'll always make it one way or another. So don't worry about it. As long as you're trying, that's all I can ever ask of you. Just keep in mind that one day when we get to where we are going; we'll remember where we've been and will appreciate it even more.

Love, Sandy

Written by: Sondra Lee Y... *February 25, 1975*

Broken Heart

As you grow up, you learn that the one person who was never supposed to let you down probably will, and will break your heart.

You will probably have your heart broken more than once, and it's harder every time.

You'll break hearts too, so remember how it felt when yours was broken.

You'll fight with your best friend. You'll blame a new love for things an old one did.

You'll cry because time is passing too fast, and you'll eventually lose someone you love.

So take too many pictures, laugh too much, and love like you've never been hurt, because every minute you spend upset is a minute of happiness you'll never get back.

Don't be afraid that your life will end,

be afraid that it will never begin.

2007

My Wish for You

To My Sweet Baby:
Whatever wish you hope comes true…
Tell me and I'll wish it, too!
....
And every time I think of YOU… I lose my cool, just
because of you!
....
May all of your tomorrows be as happy as you have made
me today!
....
I should have told you that love is more than being warm
in bed…
More than an individual seeking an accomplice…
Even more than wanting to share…
I could have said that love at best is giving…
What you need to get.

I love you much more than I can ever show you.

Sondra Lee Y…, 1976

Forgive My Heart

Forgive my heart, my foolish heart…I'm still in love with you.

Forgive my lips, if now and then, they speak your name in vain.

If you are still my only thrill, am I the only one to blame?

Forgive my dreams, in all my dreams it seems your face appears…
Forgive my eyes…I realize I'm only wasting tears…

I don't know why you haunt me, but you do…

Forgive my heart, my foolish heart; it won't believe we're through…
Forgive my heart; you're still a part of everything I do.

1960s

The Mind's Eye

We are not two jigsaw pieces under the label "couple"…you are not my other half…for society will never allow this. I see you as a woman with many changing faces…sometimes a distant rainbow fish…I watch in fascination…sometimes a star-lit sky…which I watch with a twinkle in my eye. Sometimes an octopus…with many arms that scare and entice me…

I think there is no other way to love you than to know that total vulnerability may descend at any moment. Tears on top of toughness, I sit here now with sweet memories of your soft dark skin and our minds touching each other.

1978

Pity Me Not

Pity me not because the light no longer shines for me…or at close of day…no longer shine the stars…they have all faded away.

Pity me not for beauty thus passed away…nor that my desire is hushed so soon in a sea of distain.
I know-I have for a while-you no longer look upon me with love…

Love is no more than a feeling in your heart…that your mind will not let go.
Pity me not that my heart is slow to learn…what my mind beholds at every turn.

For it is my mind I push, not my heart…maybe both are slow to learn.

1970

The Beautiful In Life...

Some talk of it in poetry,

Some grow it from the soil,

Some build it in a steeple,

Some show it through their toil,

Some show it through music,

Some mold it into art,

Some shape it into bread loaves...

Some hold it in their hearts.

For all you are, for all you do,

May everything beautiful in life come to you.

Happy Birthday, Love Sandy
October 16, 1975

Love Is For Me

The Academy Awards Goes To You, Chris
Direction…
Understanding…
Going out of your way to please me,
The willingness to change,
The ambition to do anything,
The unbelievable capacity to love,
You have the prettiest eyes I have ever seen-
And the prettiest mouth I have ever kissed.

Sondra L. Y..., June 1975

How Much for Love?

I was yours until the night was over…

Then joy faded away, and I was yours until the break of day.

Where were you when I reached out and felt the emptiness…?

Where were you when I cried out your name to be held…?

Where were you in the silence of my communication…?

I wondered where you were in our last minutes…

I spent the time watching clouds as you rode away with your important person.

Save our last minutes forever and remember how you spent them.

Weekends passing by Mondays, saying sad good-byes

Alone in a bed, the words have been said…

How much for love…each night I pretend the joy will never end.

But then the next day arrives, and again I hear you say…

How much for love…do I need to give?

1978

Here I Am

What will you look like in the morning when I finally meet you?

Sleepy eyes, rubbed red by fingers, and bright sun.

Your skin made of black silk from the moon's glow.

Your curly hair, tangled by soft pillows and happy dreams…

What will you look like when I meet my next true love…

When I see you stretch your arms…what are you reaching for…

Life…

Love…

Here I am!

1995

Tick –Tock

Minutes tick …hours tick …

Sometimes, days go by.

Waiting for that warm look…for that warm touch...

A word spoken with thought of one…you…and I!

Let's not talk of people - not our work - not what's going to be…

But about us and what is now!

What is it that I look for…what is that touch…

What is that spoken word that I am always looking for?

Will someone please tell me…who can I trust?

1977

Alone Again

This sickness I call love, I have it for you…

I can't blame you for not wanting it…

I don't want it myself.

That's why I give it so freely to people who

don't have any of their own to share.

I cannot predict what I will be,

I can only live who and what I am.

My days have been lengthened recently,

for your presence is gone from my seeing eyes.

And I am left alone, once again!

1978

The Christmas Story

She asked me what I wanted for Christmas, and I thought and wondered, and reflected over us together for these many years.

Then I realized what I wanted for Christmas was what we had in the beginning…
She asked me what I wanted for Christmas, and it's really quite simple, I just wanted the woman I met, no more, no less.

How do you tell a woman what you want for Christmas…is her love?

1992

Forever's End

It was on that magical night, when something finally went right, and love showed us its light.

It was a pleasure to have you around, a few days after we were found. Seeing you made my eyes open wide; we were ready for this magical ride.

I knew I wanted you in my life, no matter how bumpy it might be, or where it might lead.

***

Forever and always, a promise I make to you, though our future seems to be unknown…this one thought stays with me…we are not alone!

Our storybook ending I would like to be told…when we are very old…you are love…my life…my best friend. Together I hope we will reach the face of forever's end!

2006

What is Love?

Love is a feeling that never dies and can never be hidden from one's eye…

I am in love, and I shake when I try to describe the feelings I have…

But it is beyond words that can be written, though many people have tried.

It wakes me up in the morning, and puts me to sleep at night.

That person in my life will be my life…

And this means more than the world can say in words!

This is because loving someone is my life!

1967

If I Knew

If I knew how to write a song,
I'd write one everyday-
It would say that I'm falling in love with you
And why I feel this way.

It would have to say you're gorgeous,
And as rare as a desert rose;
It would say you're a looker
From your head down to your toes.
You are intelligent, courageous, funny, and fun to be with-
And as feminine as can be and way, way better than me.
You're smart, charming, and lovely;
And you're already everything to me-
You're my comfort when I'm lonely…
You're my peace when I need rest.

Of all the women I've known,
I must rate you my life's very best.
You're the orchard in the jungle;
You're the better half of me,
The half that has been missing in my life-
In a world of sometimes….misery.

You're all of this and so much more,
And already….you mean the world to me;
And I dare say…..You take my breath away!

There is still so much left unsaid,
It would take me far too long
To tell you now….how very much I care.
I would write the song and it would say…
My love for you is growing strong….with each and every day!

And if I may be so presumptuous to say…
What you have shown me up to now says that
You may feel some of what the song would say!
But the song I would write
Would be how I feel….and all about you!
And the whys…*we were meant to be*!
If I knew…how to write a song!

Your Friend, Your Love, and your Lover, for as long as you want me.

2006

Just My Thoughts of You

It's amazing how I feel when I'm around you...
How my heart pounds when you come into a room.
I look at you and think: My God!
How lovely!
And everything I am bursts into bloom.

I feel as though you must…be mine,
Not as a possession but a need, a want, a treasure….
Something almost unimaginable:
The free devotion of another soul.

As though I were about to enter heaven,
Or just within the hour be condemned to die,
My mind with one fierce thought keeps running over,
With you, and only you, I am the reason why.

I'm here……My Love is yours

Take what you will!

2006

My Love's Passion

I'm leaving you…oh my desire, my love…
And my desire has flown like a dream,
But I must stay to love another day…
And will not follow you in your life's dream.

But with me, my passion for your passion and love will
stay,
Kiss me once again, the last long kiss,
Until I draw your soul within my lips,
I want to drink down all the passion you have to
give…into my soul!

1986

Felicia

I missed your birthday because you had not come to me
yet!
On that day I was still wishing to find you!
Of all the things I wish for you,
There would not be enough paper to write it!
So I will try and show you each and every day…with
everything I do!
There has been only one true happiness in my life…that is
to love and be loved too.
You are now my life's happiness!
Thank you for coming into my life!

2006

Where Have All the Butterflies Gone?[3]

This story was written because I found another butterfly; and her name is Felicia.

Her name was Helene. Giving happiness to others was her life. She had seven children. Six girls survived, one boy died at three months old. She loved, cared for, nurtured and supported all of her girls to adulthood and beyond. She was a strong vibrant woman who loved music, singing and having fun, but most of all, she enjoyed making others happy. Everyone who met her loved her, no exceptions. In 1985, she had a stroke which left her paralyzed on the right side of her body and unable to talk. She also lost some of her short term memory and comprehension. She survived on this earth another ten years for her children. I know because I had begged her to do so when she was giving up on life. I agonized for ten years over the fact that she could not do any of the things she loved doing in life before her stroke. But she still had her beautiful smile and showed it to everyone who walked into the room she was in. It was the last day of our mother's life, December 1994 when I walked into her hospice room. I saw my sister first; Evelyn, who had been by our mother's side for twenty-four hours a day the last four weeks of our mother's life.

My mother had been taken very far away from me, and I had driven many miles from home and work to see her as often as I could. I sat with my sister, and we watched our mother in agonizing pain until about 10:00 PM. I had to go home; I had to go to work the next day. My mother was not responsive, but that was okay, I knew she felt my sister and me there next to her. My sister would be there another night, so I asked her if she needed anything. She said no, and I left.

On the way home, I did what I usually did, talked to myself and cried. I was tired and angry at all the pain my mother has had to endure all her life, even now. She did not deserve any pain! Yet

---

[3] This short story is also included in my book "Abducted Alien: A True Story of United States Immigration", which is tentatively scheduled for mid 2008 publication.

she always had a smile for others to the end. I fell right to sleep when I got home. I normally do not dream, but I did that night and remembered what it was about when I woke up when the phone rang in the middle of the night,. It was Evelyn; our mother was gone.

Before I left for the hospice, my partner Joanne told me the dream she just had. It was of my mother smiling and dancing in a beautiful dress full of butterflies. Joanne described the dress and all the colors in the dress. She also told me a lot of people were standing around my mother smiling at her. Joanne had never before seen the dress that my mother was wearing in her dream. Nor had she ever seen my mother dance. I got dressed and headed back to the hospice.

I had a smile on my face and I was trying to sing the songs my mother always sang so beautifully during her life, just like an angel. You see, the dream I had was of my mother dancing and smiling with the dress I had bought her for a trip we had recently taken together with my sister Evelyn to Las Vegas. Her family and friends who had passed on before her were standing all around her smiling.

When I walked into the hospice room, my sister was sitting next to our mother's bed, crying. I looked at my mother; she had a smile on her face. I started crying, not for my mother, but for me, for her children and everyone else she left behind. She was gone from this earth but not from our minds and hearts! We are part of her and her legacy. I will continue to look for the butterflies in this life because of my mother, Helene and my sister Evelyn who cared for her with undying love.

Chris the "Abducted Alien", December 5, 2006

Since I Met You

I have not written to you or about you for several days now.

What should I write about?

How the sunrise is more beautiful than I have ever remembered it…

How the flowers smell sweeter in the morning dew…

How your eyes raise my blood to its boiling point when you look at me…

How everything in my life has come alive and real since I met you, my love…

What can I say that I have not said, written or thought everyday since I met you…?

I Love You…

I never want to lose this feeling and hope and pray that you feel it too!

To Felicia, 2007

She

She walks in beauty like the night…under cloudless, starry skies…

And all that is best of dark and light meet in her mind, and in her eyes.

Where light sweetly expresses her thoughts,

On that cheek, so soft, and warm…the smile that wins the things she wants…

With a heart of love and innocence.

To Sharon A…, 1967

Love Is ...

Love is the greatest feeling,
Love is like a play,
Love is what I feel for you,
Each and every day,
Love is like a smile,
Love is like a song,
Love is a great emotion,
That keeps us going strong,
I love you with my heart,
My body and my soul,
I love the way I keep loving you,
Like a love I cannot control,
So remember when your eyes meet mine,
I love you with all my heart,
And I have poured my entire soul into you,
Right from the very start.

Year Unknown

We Is Friends!

Me And You Is Friends...

You Smile, I Smile....

You Hurt, I Hurt.....

You Cry, I Cry.....

You Jump Off A Bridge.....

I Gonna Miss Your E-Mails!

2006

A Special World

A special world for you and me,
A special bond one cannot see;
It wraps us up in its cocoon
and holds us fiercely in its womb.

Its fingers spread like fine spun gold,
gently nestling us into the fold…
like silken thread it holds us fast-
Bonds like this are meant to last.

And though at times a thread may break
a new one forms in its wake…
to bind us closer and keep us strong,
in a special world, where we belong.

2003

A life in harmony with nature, the love of truth and virtue,

will purge the eyes to understanding her text.

Ralph Waldo Emerson

One Heart

My love, I have tried with my entire being-
to grasp a form comparable to your own…
but nothing seems worthy.

I know now why Shakespeare could not
compare his love to a summer's day.
It would be a crime to denounce the beauty
of such a creature as you…
to simply cast away the precision
God had placed in forging you.

Each facet of your being
whether physical or spiritual,
is an ensnarement
from which there is no release.
But I do not wish release.
I wish to stay entrapped forever.

With you for all eternity, and
our hearts as one.

2006

What I Love About You

I love the way you look at me,
your eyes so bright and sunset brown.
I love the way you kiss me,
your lips so soft and smooth.

I love the way you make me happy,
and the ways you show you care.
I love the way you say, "I Love You,"
And the way you're always there…

I love the way you touch me,
always sending chills down my spine.
I love that you are with me…
And I'm glad that you are now my shining light.

A gentle word like a spark of light,
Illuminates my soul--
And as each sound goes deeper inside,
it's *you* that makes me whole.

There is no corner, no dark place,
your love cannot fill;
And if the world starts causing waves,
It's your devotion that makes them still.

And yes, you always speak to me,
In sweet honesty and truth-
Your caring heart keeps out the rain;
your love is the ultimate roof.

So thank you my Love for being there,
for supporting me, my life -
I'll do the same for you, you know,
with undying love for life!
Chris the Abducted Alien, 2006

October's Party

October gave a party...
The leaves by the hundreds came,
The ash, oak, and maple...
And those of every name.

The sunshine spread a carpet,
And everything was grand;
Miss Weather led the dancing,
Professor Wind the band.

The chestnuts came in yellow,
The oak in crimson dressed,
The lovely Miss Maple,
In scarlet looked her best;

All balanced to their partners,
They gaily fluttered by,
The sight was like a rainbow,
New fallen in the sky.

Then in the rustic billows,
At "Hide and Seek" they played,
The party closed at sundown,
And everybody stayed;

Professor Wind played louder,
They flew along the ground,
And here the party ended,
In jolly "All Hands Round".

Chris the Abducted Alien, 1959
1st Place Winner

My Goodbye

There are many things in our past, that at various times I felt were not cohesive to our relationship together (I'm talking about our personalities, our friends, our life style, etc.). I did not care, and my position in our relationship was not to change you, and I have tried to the best of my ability to change myself for you. It was only to accept everything that you are and have become as a person through your life experiences that I have tried to love you. But you would not allow me to love, even though all I wanted to do…was make you smile.

Chris the Abducted Alien, 2005

To Master Love

I don't expect you soon to love me true...
But my own feelings are very clear.
Passion is the lonesome entrance-
To a world we crave and fear.

We cannot know where this will take us...
Nor whether we will ride for long,
but our happiness and our pleasure is the overture
that flows into the longer concert song.

So come with me with open mind and heart,

And our laughter with joy unfettered…

And we with time will prove…
perhaps, someday with unending love...

We might Master it together...

Chris the Abducted Alien, 2002

I Will Surrender Only To You

My love for you is a song that goes on forever,
my love has been a prisoner, and only to you I will
surrender.

I love you deeply; I love you so much,
I love the sound of your voice
And the way you touch every part of my being....
The joy you bring me, is my reason for living,
this is how it has been from the start...
When I first saw your incredibly, beautiful eyes.

When I am with you, eternity is a step away...
My love continues to grow each and every passing day...
A treasure of love you have given me, and I have found in
only you...
I never really felt before now or maybe I have forgotten
how...
but it is because of you I do again...
give you my love, which has always been only mine to
give.

It is something I cherish deep within my soul...
And how much I love you...
and the wanting you to know...
this has been my life's only meaning...
my life's only goal...
until I find the gold at the end of the rainbow...
Now I know; the gold I have found in you.

Each facet of your being,
Whether physical or spiritual,
is an ensnarement of all my feelings...
of which there is no release.
And of which I do not want release.

I wish to stay entrapped in my love for you forever.

I wish to be with you for all eternity.
Our hearts are already one…
And there *is* no possible separation because you are the one…

If I could have one wish,
I would wish to wake up everyday
To the sound of your breath on my neck,
The warmth of your lips on my cheek,
The touch of your fingers on my skin,
The feel of your heart beating with mine…
Knowing I could never find this feeling with anyone but you…

I love the way you make me so happy,
And the ways you show me you care…
I love the way you say, "I Love You,"
And the way you are always right there.

I love the way you touch me,
Always a warm and affectionate caress,
That always sends chills down my spine.
And the ache I feel, when my love comes down…
It's because I want you so much!

I love that you are with me,
No matter where we are,
It's you, who has made me whole,
It's you, who has stopped the aching deep in my soul
It's that gentle spark of light,
That always illuminates my soul,
And as it goes deeper; again I'm aware
That it's you who makes us one with the universe…
Together we are whole!

I think of you each morning,
And dream of you each night,
I dream of your arms around me,
And always express my delight…
Never have I fallen…nor do I feel
I will ever love another…
You have given your love to me, like no other….
It is your love that makes my love stronger…
Our love has a chance to last forever…

I have said some of these words to another…
but the feeling was only within me and not the other…
for you Felicia will always be part of me, my soul and my reality!
For you have given me a part of you…
It's most secret part, your love to treasure!

I do not want to mar this love I have for you with any doubts…
but it has always been you in control of our destiny…
And it is what I have always feared…
But your love of me has shown me, and my fear has disappeared.

My love for you is a song, which goes on forever,
My love is a prisoner; it's only to you that I will surrender!

My testament of love to Felicia:
Chris the "Abducted Alien", 2006

MY ANGEL, MY CONFUSION

An angel was on my shoulder the night I met you, and I will never forget!
More than fate brought us together…I feel you were and are the one…
I have been waiting for my whole life, whether in karma, or in thought.

This I have always believed is true. You were and are my guiding light.
You always guided me through the toughest of times into the most recent phase of my life.

You were always by my side, even through the ugliest and hardest times…
It was you who was the first to add meaning to my life…you who made my whole world shine.
You are the wind beneath my wings…the air that I breathe, you are the best part of my heart, and the best part of me.

You always seemed to find a way to make me laugh and smile and turn my darkest days bright. When I was in a spiraling fall ….you made my whole life worthwhile

I will treasure everything we had and all the moments that we shared…
I'm glad you came into my life and, most importantly, that you cared.

You taught me what true happiness is, and you taught me to feel true pain too.
The real meaning of love is you don't give up…which I have seemed always to do.

You have been my dream come true among all others I have known, and I am the one that gave up on you. And the why is still unknown.
What is it about me, that fatal flaw in my character?

My life is nothing without you…right now I feel that it never will be…or is my mind detached from knowing what will come to pass?

You are the meaning of *ME*, and always will be…
or is there another in the shadows waiting for me?

To give up an angel that I adore…to give up my life, because I cannot change!

What is it about me, that fatal flaw?

You say you have moved on-
I say okay, and the pain begins, but I will not forget-
I say okay, and the pain persists, but I will continue to fight for your heart-
I say okay, and the pain remains, but my heart is still yours, and the way I feel right now, always will be…or is my mind detached from my heart--saying you will be?

Today, tomorrow, and forever, because I will not forget!
Because you truly are, the better part of what I call *ME*.

To give up an angel, an angel I adore, angel sent from above, just for me is the cruelest thing I could have done to myself.

And all because I say, I cannot change!
Please forgive *ME*!

And please believe me when I say…

I am and always will be here for you...even as I take my last breath and then beyond.
Or are these words being prepared for another?

My heart is heavy with pain for you, with what I have done to you.
And pain for the wanting of you and your love--

All because I say, I cannot change! But why should I--I did not ask for you to change...?

And I truly feel ashamed...
Please, please forgive *ME*!

Chris the Abducted Alien, 2005

To Sandy

Awake or asleep...I carry this dream of you and in some beautiful way it keeps reminding me of you...how much sweeter my life has been because you were a part of it...now and forever...

Chris the "Abducted Alien"

Silence

The music in my heart I hear....
As I listen to the silence of the night....
Long after the sound disappears...
My mind envisions the sound of your laughter...
The look of your smile...
Your breath against my neck...
How could I ever forget you?
I will until love returns!

Chris the Abducted Alien, Year Unknown

My Daddy

As I sit watching by your bed, a million thoughts run through my head.

Just how much are you aware?
Do you know that I am here?
Can you feel the love I am sending…?
In whispered word, or prayer lent?

Upon my cross, I ask God to spare your life for my selfish cause,
so that I can tell you just once more..."I Love You Daddy"…
We could chat like days of old, over coffee cups all rimmed with gold!
We could laugh and joke, or just share some small hurt and perhaps a tear talking of the past, or things yet to do...
To sniffle and sneeze and say, "Bless you"...
All these dreams now hang in shreds as I sit here
with bowed head and live with these sad thoughts.

Monique Cheri J..., 2003

You Are the One Who

Sweetheart, you are my heart's true love….
The one I was meant to meet across time…

Across space and whatever obstacles life put in our way!

You are the one I am meant to be beside now and
forever…
The one whose kiss is magic to me…
The one whose eyes reach into my soul…
The one whose laughter lights my day…
And whose whispers of caring warm my nights…

You are the one who understands what's in my heart…
The one in whose arms I share refuge from the world and
all its cares…

You are the one with whom I find such a deep wonderful
and exciting love!
I am so glad to be sharing life's beautiful adventures with
you!

Chris the Abducted Alien, Year Unknown

The Wind, the Sand, and the Sky

I wrote your name in the sky,

But the wind blew it away.

I wrote your name in the sand,

But the waves washed it away.

I wrote your name in my heart,

And forever it will stay.

We have fallen and were hurt,

We have loved and know now it might continue,

For true love continues, and this I have learned,

I will try until I get it right,

And I will never give up,

For our destiny is in our hands.

The thoughts in your mind,

Which are sometimes never spoken will lead us

To our life's destiny,

And my thoughts have always been of you since our first

rendezvous!

Let's try again, until we get it right!

2002

Dwelling on Past Pain

Heartbreak and loss leave you vulnerable to further attack
and will reopen old wounds.
It can ultimately consume you…particularly when it is
your own heart that is betraying you.

Thoughts of getting even will make things even worse.
Taking each betrayal and loss too personally becomes a
self-fulfilling prophecy....

So when you do finally let your guard down and trust
again,
You find yourself embroiled in the same emotional drama
you vowed to avoid.
Being on the defensive and carrying a chip on your
shoulder practically ensures tension and wounded pride,
and your self-esteem may suffer as a result.

Certain loss is irrevocable.

Author Unknown

Happiness Is the Road

For the longest time, it seemed that life was about to start. Real LIFE! But there was always some obstacle along the way, an ordeal to get through, some work to be finished, some time to be given, bills to be paid......Then life would really start.

I finally came to understand that those obstacles are life. Your life will always be full of challenges.

Chris the "Abducted Alien" 2007

Music is the only language in which you cannot say a mean or sarcastic thing.

Lord Erskine

Boy was he wrong! Unless he was talking about music without words!!!

Chris the "Abducted Alien", 2006

My Feelings

My feelings for you have always touched my heart immensely, giving a great deal of pain to me when I could not be with you, or even the fact that I no longer made you happy or could make you smile. I did not and do not like that pain, but sometimes it is needed to move on. The pain never went away in me, I never let you go; you were always with me day and night, no matter where I was or who I was with.

But like pain does, it eventually goes away, but the memory of…will always stay.

Chris the Abducted Alien, 2005

She Is More Than a Lover

She is more than a lover…she is a goddess in my eyes. The woman who allows me to sit beside her…who listens intimately to the sweet murmur of my voice…her enticing laughter that makes my own heart beat fast. If I meet you suddenly, I can't speak…my tongue is broken. A thin flame runs under my skin…seeing nothing, hearing nothing…only my ears drumming. I drip with sweat…trembling shakes my body and my heart is about to burst.

At such times, I feel that death is not far from me…yet I live on giving love…hoping one day soon…that same love will be returned.

Chris the Abducted Alien, Year Unknown

Love's Sacrifice

Sometimes, I think that I would gladly sacrifice twenty-five years of life for but a moment to love.

The barrier which separates us is not of external origin…but exists only in our minds…mine!
I have tried many times without success to break through this wall.

I shall try again harder than ever before. But pain inflicted in youth creates walls of steel that give the illusion of coldness and indifference.

When in truth that which lies behind the wall is pure, unselfish and never ending love…for one, and only one individual, of whose choosing I know not.

But if I do have a choice, I choose you.

Childhood nightmares are difficult to overcome; especially when they cannot be remembered.

I can say no more that would make sense to you except, perhaps, if I could exchange feelings with you I would gladly do so.

For being capable of loving someone is truly a far greater thing than to be destined to live a life filled only with experiences.

As a poet once said, *"It is better to have loved and lost, than to have never loved at all."*

Written by: Sondra L. Y…, 1974

Pity Me Not

Weeping my love, there…there…you cannot know what waits for you…how it will be…falling…down, down, down…all broken.
And none to pity but me…kiss me…never again.
Come closer, closer…hold my hand…no!
Put your arms around me…now kiss me…lips to lips…never again…no!

1969

Anguished Love

One of the saddest facts about love and falling in love…it is not always mutual. When you are terribly fond of another person who does not even seem aware of your existence…does not return your affection…you can go through torture.
When in spite of all your efforts, the one you adore does not return your affection, there is nothing sensible that you can do except get over the stormy love that wracks your present life…do not take it out on any future love.

2001

Soupir d'amour (Whisper of Love)

And I can never forget you…
You shall see that a more enduring love than mine never had existence…
Triumph over fate securing…death shall yield to its resistance.

Sorrow

What sorrow is there that has not been mine…lover lost and friends gone.
We stand at the same point of pain…you call to me with your tears…and I come.
What more is there?

Time to Go

If you go away, as I know you will, you must tell the world to stop turning until you return again, if you ever do. For what good is love, without you…can I tell you now as you turn to go, I'll be dying slow, until the next hello? If you go away, on this summer day, then you might as well take the Sun away, and all the birds that flew in the summer sky…when our love was new and our hearts were high…as the day was young…as we started our journey of love.

But if you stay, I'll make you a night, like no night has been, or will be again. We will ride on the Sun…ride on the rain…talk to the trees…and worship the clouds. But if you go, there will be nothing left…no one to trust…just an empty room full of empty space…like the empty look I see on your face.

I look at you…that is all I dare to do…for you go your way…as I must go mine. We may greet while passing…but our moments are numbered. For I am not brave enough to chance another trip of love that will be only in my mind…so I'll let you go…touch me one more time…let me see your smile…let me dream my dream.

What hurts more, pride or rejection? So I scream that I will not have you treat me this way…when you have…I will…and do.

And yes, I know it's time to go…so I am begging you to give me something which you do not have to give…and yes, I know it's time to go.

You sit and stare at me…you ask what I am thinking…I say someone will be hurt soon…you do not know the time has come to go…and end a love that never was.

Chris the Abducted Alien, Year Unknown

Dion (Darlene)
Dedicated to our Family and Friends

For those I love and those who love me.
You must not grieve because I have gone.

Release me and let me fly.
Let my spirit soar upon your love to the sky.

You were each an integral part of my life on earth,
As such our spirits joined, an exchange was made,
I shall remain in your hearts forever.

Release me and let me fly,
Let my spirit soar upon your love to the sky.
Love bridges time and space;
When you need me,
Open the door in your heart: I'll be there.

For now,
Rejoice as you release me to let me fly.
Let my spirit soar…upon your love to the sky.

This is perfect; it sounds just like Darlene, my friend eternally! This is her eulogy by her sister (Author Unknown) Diane T. K. and Darlene's friends.

Shari

God set her brave eyes wide apart…and painted them
with fire,
They stir the ashes of my heart to ambers of desire.

Her hands are soft…with the voice of an angel…
when I see her move towards me…
I know in every truth that…I will not die for less than
love.

Ah, dear precious lovely thing…your eyes, I have sought
them like prayer…
they are eyes that I have longed for and desired.

And in my dreams you are my ecstasy and my
desire…but you love another…
so only my dreams are my desire and my fantasy…
but they still are the eyes of Shari.

To Sharon A…, 1966

Fulfilled

You just can't imagine how much I miss you sometimes.
Often it seems like forever before we have a chance to get together.

But when we finally do it's like I felt when I first met you.
Life is a journey that has been so much easier with you by my side.

We have to be apart…
I know this now.

But thoughts of you are never far from my mind.
I appreciate everything you are…
and everything you do.
I am here because of you.

Chris the "Abducted Alien"

Deep Breath

Applause will die away!
Trophies will gather dust!
Winners are soon forgotten!

Happiness is a voyage, not a destination.
There is no better time to be happy than NOW!
Live and enjoy the moment.

Take a deep breath and…just be.

Chris the "Abducted Alien"

Because of You

As I sit here bored and don't feel like talking to the people here...
I don't feel like looking at this place anymore...
I sit here lonely realizing that it's not people or places that make me happy...
It's you!
If you have a goal in life that takes a lot of energy, that incurs a great deal of interest, and that is a challenge to you, you will always look forward to waking up to see what the new day brings.

If you find a person in your life who understands you completely who shares your ideas and who believes in everything you do, you will always look forward to the night because you will never be lonely.

[I love you and I think I understand you (sometimes),
Love Sandy (Written 1974)]

If I had a choice to live without loving...I would choose not to live!

Chris the Abducted Alien, 2007

The Voice of a Friend (Trees of Life)

I have never been a religious person; however, I have always enjoyed reading passages in the Bible and have believed in some of the writing within because it speaks to our souls. It allows us the opportunity to mold ourselves into what we are today. It is up to each of us to pick our paths in life; but sometimes our paths are picked for us, without control as to what we can do, or what is done to us. Our lives will always be full of challenges. This is *life*! Find happiness whenever you can and believe in yourself and in your strength, no matter what path has been given to you to follow!

Chris the Abducted Alien, 2007

Ode to My Family

Nothing in the *world* can take the place of persistent and caring family members.

Talent will not[4];
Nothing is more common than unsuccessful men/women with talent.

Genius will not;
Unrewarded genius is almost a proverb.

Education will not;
The world is full of educated people who are derelicts, that don't care about anyone or anything but themselves.

Persistence and determination alone are omnipotent.

It is because of my two cousin's persistence and caring that my soul is at ease.

My gratitude is beyond words-

Thank You.

Chris the Abducted Alien, June 2, 2007

---

[4] Quotes by Calvin Coolidge, 1830s.

You and I

You and I are connected
in a way that goes beyond romance...
beyond friendship,
beyond what we've ever had before.
It has defied time and distance...
and changes in ourselves,
and in our lives.

It has defied every explanation.
Except one:
Pure and simple, we're soul mates.

I can't explain...I just feel it.
It's there in the way my spirits lift
whenever we talk.

The sound of your voice brings me to places
I have missed and did not know.

It's in the delight I feel, when we laugh
at exactly the same things we like and don't like.

When I'm with you it's like a tiny piece of the
Universe shifts into place.

A place it's supposed to be.
I have not been there for a very long time.
All is now right with the world because of you.

These things, and so many more,
have made me understand
that this is a once in a lifetime...
forever connection.
And Yes, in so short a time!

This connection that could only exist between you and me--
Deep within my soul, I know that our relationship
is a rare gift sent to us from our friends…
one that will bring us extraordinary happiness--
all through our lives.

Please let it be, come back to me!

Chris the Abducted Alien

Rebound Lover

Our feelings about a person we love cannot be controlled. Our minds can tell us that one affair is over, but our feelings for them are still there. What we wanted out of this broken first relationship is in our haunting dreams continuously. It is not anyone's fault if you have never experienced this type of feeling and have allowed another to fall in love with you, this is natural.

It would only be your fault knowing, before the fact, when the person you have always dreamed of comes into your life, and you try to make it work. Knowing that you are still in love with the person you left, or who left you. The rebound relationship (us) is disastrous for both and just a matter of time before this relationship also will be over because of doubt, which eventually turns to dislike of the other.

There were times in my life that this was the reverse, and I was not ready. But I continued the relationship anyway. I was allowed this experience much earlier than you. And I, different from you, went into the relationship knowing this, and in turn, the other person was hurt because of me.

Either way our relationship will never work in its existing form. There can be only one love in your heart and mind; at any one time in your life.

Wanting a true love in our lifetime is what every person dreams. Wanting someone you know will be there for you no matter what, care for you, treat you with respect, and love you unconditionally. And in turn you are there for them. I truly feel you have met that person in me, and I have met that person in you, but you are not ready.

Some have achieved this satisfaction in their lives where both are free to love. Many others never do. They continue to search their entire lives without the true contentment of what is called *TRUE LOVE*. This type of loving of two people is mutual knowing and trusting that it will always be there. Your love, your one and only, always will be there through the good and bad times.

To continue a rebound relationship is certain disaster. You would hurt that person more by continuing the relationship. You must complete one relationship in order to be truly free to love another. This is just a fact, and you cannot control it. I know, I have hurt many people like this and have paid dearly for it in any future relationships by having the same done to me.

This is called Karma, and I truly believe in it!

You must finish one relationship for the other to survive and bloom, not wither and die. You must return to the first love until you know for sure. There can be no thoughts that the first relationship is over, and it will be over, because this type of relationship never works either.

There was a reason that the first relationship did not continue, and you have just forgotten the why because you loved this person very much, and you wanted to do everything in your power to make it work. The reason why it did not work in the first place will return to you only if you continue the relationship to its completion. If you do not do this, there will always be doubts, and no other relationship that you have, has a chance to survive.

You must return to your first love, no matter what form or manner this takes, and continue this relationship to its conclusion.

I love you without reserve, and I will be here waiting for you to return to me. But you must only do this if you are ready to be here just for me. I would not be able to live with the thought of you loving someone else, or even not knowing if you do or not. My love for you will survive whatever you must do, no matter how long it takes.

When I met you my heart was finally free to love, yours was not. Again, it was not your fault, but mine. This has been my entire life, a continuous circle of love events like this that have never ended. I knew this coming into our relationship, and took the chance anyway. This was my choice, not yours.

Now knowing the person you are, I know that you had no clue what you were feeling when you saw your first love again after many months of not seeing her or maybe even talking to her.

I did feel this in you and I was worried a lot about this possibility being one of the reasons for your distress over the past several months. That is why I asked you before you left if your friend was going to be going with you to the family reunion. This is why I forced myself not to make contact with you after you left that message on my phone. But I could not stop myself from wanting to see you again, so I called you. And probably will not be able to stop myself in the future from calling you again. Please allow me this indiscretion whenever you can, knowing that it will hurt you to see me, as it will, me seeing you.

I truly believe you when you say you love me. I am easy to love; I have been this way all my life, people love me because of who I am. But it is not the type of love that I need from a person that I want to spend the rest of my life with. Again, none of this is your fault, so stop trying to take the blame for something you had no control over.

Let us try to do this so our love for one another survives this new life experience for you. I have been there many times. And even though I have, it does not make it hurt any less, it was my choice to fall in love with you, knowing that this might occur; please remember this.

I still want us to spend the rest of our lives together. I am hoping that this will not take too long. Again, this is only how I feel, not what you should do to make our love survive. So when I tell you I understand, I am telling you a lot without saying anything.

Chris the Abducted Alien

Come to the End of Words[5]

Nothing less than the undivided universe can be our true home. Yet how can one speak or even think about the whole of things? Language is of only modest help. Every sentence is a wispy net, capturing a few flecks of meaning. The sun shines without vocabulary. The salmon has no name for the urge that drives it upstream. The newborn groping for the nipple knows hunger long before it knows a single word. Even with an entire dictionary in one's head, one eventually comes to the end of words. Then what? Then drink deep like the baby, swim like the salmon, burn like any brief star.

Scott Russell Sanders

Author, title, and publisher Beacon Press
Copyright © 1993

Breathe deeply and listen only to the Angels
in the universe!

---

[5] From Staying Put: Making a Home in a Restless World by Scott Russell Sanders, Copyright ©1993 by Scott Russell Sanders.

Till We Meet Again...
My Family...My Heart

Helene H...1994   Sandra Y...2000
Marcia C...2001   Raymond J...2002
Glodien T...2002   Dion (Darlene) T...2003
Dorothy M...2003   Renée J...2003
Gilberte R...2006 John Louie R...2006
Lisette G...2005   Giles B...abt. 1997

Prayer of St. Francis of Assisi

Make me an instrument of peace;
Where there is hatred, let me sow love;
Where there is injury, pardon;
Where there is doubt, faith;
Where there is despair, hope;
Where there is darkness, light; and
Where there is sadness, joy!
Grant that I may not so much seek to be consoled as to console;
To be understood as to understand;
To be loved as to love; for it is pardoning that we are pardoned,
And it is in dying that we are born to eternal life!

Credits and Sources

1. Excerpt from newspaper article, Evansville, Indiana (USA). Sondra Lee Y… (Born: 1950 – Died: June 4, 2000)   Sondra Lee Y…, 50, of Akron, Ohio, formerly of   Evansville, died Sunday, June 4, 2000. She was found   in her car, the coroner in Akron is investigating.
She was a licensed social worker by the state of Ohio. She was a homeless outreach specialist for the YWCA in Canton, Ohio, and had developed programs funded by the federal government to reduce the homeless population.
In 1998 she began working as an administrative assistant for Akron University.
She was a graduate of the University of Southern Indiana.

2. All original hand written poems, letters, short stories are currently in the possession of *Chris the Abducted Alien.* They have been edited for spelling and/or words only. Structure or meanings of phrases have not been changed. All letters were reproduced from the original hand-written version for input to the computer and have not been altered in meaning. Author, Chris the "Abducted Alien".

3. Reference for Creative Writing of Poems: Instant Quotation Dictionary, 1969, Compiled by Donald O. Bolander, B.S., M.A., Director of Education, Career Institute. Dolores D. Varner, Gary B. Wright, B.A., Stephanie H. Greene, Published by Career Institute, 1500 Cardinal Drive, Little Falls, New Jersey, 07424.

Credits and Sources

4. Quotes: Grateful acknowledgment is made for permission to reprint the following material from authors listed below and/or used under Open Content:
   i. Maya Angelou (1928 -) African-American, poet, educator, historian, best-selling author, actress, playwright, civil-rights activist, producer and director.
   ii. Bret Harte (1836-1902) American writer who helped create the local-colour school in American fiction.
   iii. Charles Augustus Lindbergh (1902-1974) American aviator, made the first solo nonstop flight across the Atlantic Ocean on May 20-21, 1927.
   iv. Theodore Roosevelt (1887-1944) Twenty-Sixth President of the United States (1901-1909).
   v. John Bowring (1792-1872) 4th Governor of Hong Kong (1854-1859).
   vi. Adlai E. Stevenson (1835-1914) 23rd Vice-President of the United States (1893-1897).
   vii. Calvin Coolidge (1872-1933) 30th President of the United States (1923-1929).
   viii. Scott Russell Sanders, from Staying Put: Making a Home in a Restless World,. Author, title, and publisher Beacon Press. Copyright © 1993
   ix. Eulogy (Author Unknown) Diane T. Kirtsy and Darlene's friends for a celebration of Dion's life.

5. Scott Russell Sanders quotation was first read in this book: 100 Ways to keep your Soul Alive, 1994, living deeply and fully every day / edited by Frederic Brussat and Mary Brussat. HarperCollins Publishers, Inc., 10 East 53rd Street, New York, NY 10022.

Credits and Sources

6. Message sent in this card from, Blue Mountain Arts, Inc., Thoughts of You, by Susan Polis Schultz.

7. Cover Picture: artist MDK Perkins, (Black Baby Angel) picture – www.tyy-gil.com, cover for An Angel for You "My Life in Poems, Letters & Short Stories," author/publisher Chris_the_Abducted_Alien.

8. Picture of man holding woman on second page, unknown artist, sent to me in an e-mail, could not find artist. If anyone recognizes the art please contact author/publisher at: Chris_the_Abducted_Alien@comcast.net

9. Open Content: http://wiki.creativecommons.org/Legal_Concepts

ISBN: 978-0-6151-7021-3

www.ingramcontent.com/pod-product-compliance
Lightning Source LLC
Chambersburg PA
CBHW020017050426
42450CB00005B/515